D0816641

anythink
No longer property of Anythink Libraries

Write It Right

Writing About Your Adventure

By Cecilia Minden and Kate Roth

Published in the United States of America by
Cherry Lake Publishing
Ann Arbor, Michigan
www.cherrylakepublishing.com

Reading Adviser: Marla Conn MS, Ed., Literacy specialist, Read-Ability, Inc.
Book Designer: Felicia Macheske
Character Illustrator: Carol Herring

Photo Credits: © Sunychka Sol/Shutterstock.com, 5; © OHishiapply/Shutterstock.com, 7; © Zurijeta/Shutterstock.com, 11;
© Brocreative/Shutterstock.com, 15

Graphics Throughout: © simple surface/Shutterstock.com; © Mix3r/Shutterstock.com; © Artefficient/Shutterstock.com; © lemony/
Shutterstock.com; © Svetolk/Shutterstock.com; © EV-DA/Shutterstock.com; © briddy/Shutterstock.com; © IreneArt/Shutterstock.com

Library of Congress Cataloging-in-Publication Data has been filed and is available at catalog.loc.gov

Cherry Lake Publishing would like to acknowledge the work of The Partnership for 21st Century Skills.
Please visit *www.p21.org* for more information.

Printed in the United States of America
Corporate Graphics

Table of
CONTENTS

CHAPTER ONE

Sharing Your Story

Think of the most exciting **adventure** you have ever experienced. Do you want to share your story with other people? Try writing a **personal narrative**!

A personal narrative is a story about something meaningful or special that has happened to the author. The author is represented by the pronoun I. This is called writing in the first person.

Writing a personal narrative is a good way to share your adventures with others.

CHAPTER TWO

Write About What You Know!

Your personal narrative should focus on a single experience or adventure. Look at photographs. Talk to your family and friends. Narrow down possible **topics** for your personal narrative. Choose one to bring to life for other people!

You can't include every single detail of your adventure. If you did, your personal narrative would become a list! Instead, focus on the part that is the most interesting or exciting. It is helpful to list the **events** that occurred in **chronological** order. Think of a hill. You want your personal narrative to build up to the most exciting part of your adventure. What details can you add to build up your story?

Looking at pictures will help you remember your experiences.

ACTIVITY

Plan Your Adventure Story!

HERE'S WHAT YOU'LL NEED:

- Any photographs of your adventure
- A pencil and paper (or a computer and a printer)

INSTRUCTIONS:

1. Talk to your family and friends about adventures you have shared and look at photographs of those experiences.
2. List three experiences that you would enjoy sharing with others.
3. Pick one topic to write about. Focus on the most interesting part of this adventure.
4. Now write a list of all the events that made your adventure exciting.
5. Put the list in chronological order.

Sample Topic List

- My first plane ride
- Our vacation in St. Louis, Missouri ✓
- A bike ride up a mountain

Sample List of Chronological Events

Visiting St. Louis, Missouri:

1. I went to the St. Louis Zoo with my family.
2. We started in the Butterfly Dome.
3. We walked all over the zoo in the heat.
4. Finally, we went in the Penguin House.
5. I didn't want to leave because it was nice and cool.
6. We really liked our adventure at the St. Louis Zoo.

CHAPTER THREE

How Did It Begin?

Close your eyes and think about how your adventure began. Your opening should make readers feel the same way you did at that moment. They should want to learn more about your experience after reading your opening.

What did you see, smell, hear, and feel when your adventure started? Were you excited or scared? Write a few sentences about what you experienced. Choose the one that would make the best opening!

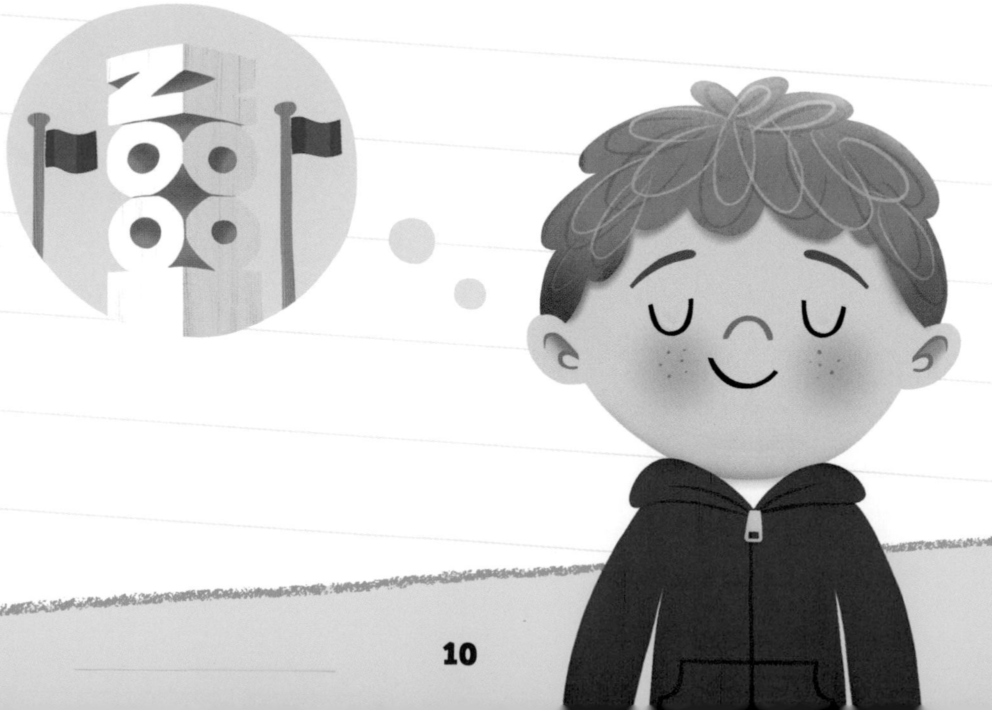

Try to remember the beginning of your adventure.

ACTIVITY

Write Your Opening!

HERE'S WHAT YOU'LL NEED:

- Any photographs of your adventure
- A pencil and paper (or a computer and a printer)

INSTRUCTIONS:

1. Think about how your adventure began. Looking at your photographs again may be helpful.
2. Write three possible openings for your story.
3. Pick the one that will make readers most interested in reading about your adventure.

OPENING IDEAS:

1. We spent our vacation in St. Louis, Missouri. I'd never been, and there was so much to do and see. The one place we all wanted to go was the St. Louis Zoo.
2. We woke up to a hot, sunny day in St. Louis, Missouri, but that wasn't going to keep us from our vacation adventure. We filled a bag with hats, sunscreen, and water bottles and set off to explore the number one zoo in the USA.
3. My whole family went on a vacation to St. Louis, Missouri, home of the number one zoo in the USA. We had many adventures, but we all agree that visiting the zoo was the best part of our trip.

CHAPTER FOUR

What Happened Next?

Now, start writing the **body** of your personal narrative. Imagine your story as a movie in your mind. What important details do you include? Keep adding details to your narrative that will help readers experience what you did. Use words like *after* and *then* to show the chronology of events. Including **dialogue** also helps bring your story to life!

Be sure to explain the main problem or situation in your adventure. As you tell your story, build toward the **climax**. The climax is the turning point just before the main problem is solved or an important event occurs.

The climax of a story is a lot like the very top of a roller coaster before a big drop.

ACTIVITY

Write the Body!

HERE'S WHAT YOU'LL NEED:

- Any photographs of your adventure
- Your list of chronological events
- A pencil and paper (or a computer and a printer)

INSTRUCTIONS:

1. Look at your photographs and list of chronological events.
2. Continue adding details to your story that build toward the climax.
3. Keep these tips in mind:
   - Keep your story focused.
   - Use words to show the passage of time.
   - Use the first person.
   - Include dialogue to help bring your adventure to life.

Sample Body

The first thing we saw at the zoo was the Butterfly Dome. If you stood very still, the butterflies would land on your arm. It was humid and shady inside, but that would soon end when we stepped out into the bright sun.

We walked for what seemed like miles in the heat. The temperature was almost 100 degrees. The zoo provided lots of water and shade for the animals. We saw elephants standing under a big waterfall. It was hard to keep from jumping in!

We were enjoying many sights, but the heat was dragging us down. We thought we would have to go home without seeing the rest of the zoo. Then Mom spotted the Penguin House. "Let's get in line," said Dad. We stood outside in the hot sun, wondering why people were taking so long to go through. Then we went inside and realized why.

CHAPTER FIVE

How Did It End?

The ending of a personal narrative includes a **resolution**. This part of the story tells how the main problem was solved or what happened after the main event occurred. It lets readers know how your adventure ended.

After you finish writing your resolution, give your personal narrative a title. Try to keep it short. Choose words that will catch readers' attention.

ACTIVITY

Write the Ending and the Title!

HERE'S WHAT YOU'LL NEED:

- Your list of chronological events
- A pencil and paper (or a computer and a printer)

INSTRUCTIONS:

1. Write the resolution to your story.
2. Read your story aloud to hear how it sounds.
3. Write three possible titles.
4. Choose the title that you think will do the best job of getting readers' attention.

Sample Ending

It was very cold in the Penguin House. It felt great. No wonder folks were taking their time! We enjoyed watching the funny penguins do their tricks. We left feeling cool and refreshed and ready to explore the rest of the zoo. We all agreed that the Penguin House was our favorite exhibit, especially on a very hot summer day.

Sample Titles

Title Ideas:

1. A Hot Time at the St. Louis Zoo
2. The Penguin House
3. Adventures with Animals

CHAPTER SIX

A Final Step Before You Share

Don't forget to reread your personal narrative before you share it with others. Check for any spelling and grammar mistakes. Do you remember other special moments that could become personal narratives?

ACTIVITY

Remember to Review!

Ask yourself these questions as you reread your personal narrative:

- Do I have an attention-getting title and opening?
- Do I show readers what I felt and experienced?
- Do I include dialogue?
- Do I use words that explain the events in chronological order?
- Do I add details that help build the story to the climax?
- Do I include a resolution in my ending?
- Do I use correct grammar and spelling?

GLOSSARY

adventure (ad-VEN-chur) a wild or exciting activity or event

body (BAH-dee) the main part of a personal narrative

chronological (krah-nuh-LAH-jih-kuhl) following the order in which events occur

climax (KLYE-maks) the turning point in a story that occurs just before the resolution

dialogue (DYE-uh-lawg) spoken words between two or more people

events (ih-VENTS) things that occur at set places and times

personal narrative (PUR-suh-nuhl NAR-uh-tiv) a first-person story about something meaningful that has happened to the author

resolution (rez-uh-LOO-shuhn) the part of a personal narrative that tells how the story ends

topics (TAH-piks) subjects

BOOKS

Fletcher, Ralph J. *How to Write Your Life Story*. New York: Collins, 2007.

Jarnow, Jill. *Writing to Retell*. New York: PowerKids Press, 2006.

WEBSITES

TIME for Kids—Personal Narrative
https://www.cbsd.org/Page/16453
Check out this site for samples of personal narratives.

INDEX

About the AUTHORS

Cecilia Minden is the former director of the Language and Literacy Program at Harvard Graduate School of Education. She earned her doctorate from the University of Virginia. While at Harvard, Dr. Minden also taught several writing courses. Her research focused on early literacy skills and developing phonics curriculums. She is now a literacy consultant and the author of over 100 books for children. Dr. Minden lives with her family in McKinney, Texas. She enjoys visiting the St. Louis Zoo.

Kate Roth has a doctorate from Harvard University in language and literacy and a master's degree from Columbia University Teachers College in curriculum and teaching. Her work focuses on writing instruction in the primary grades. She has taught kindergarten, first grade, and Reading Recovery. She has also instructed hundreds of teachers from around the world in early literacy practices. She lived with her husband and three children in China for many years, and now they live in Connecticut.